TAKE IT TO THE LIMIT
STUDY GUIDE

TAKE IT
TO THE
LIMIT

STUDY GUIDE

ANDY STANLEY

Multnomah® Publishers *Sisters, Oregon*

TAKE IT TO THE LIMIT STUDY GUIDE
published by Multnomah Publishers, Inc.

© 2005 by North Point Ministries, Inc.
International Standard Book Number: 1-59052-550-7

Cover design by Andrew Cochran at Circle@Seven Studio

Unless otherwise indicated, Scripture quotations are from:
The Holy Bible, New International Version
© 1973, 1984 by International Bible Society,
used by permission of Zondervan Publishing House

Multnomah is a trademark of Multnomah Publishers, Inc.,
and is registered in the U.S. Patent and Trademark Office.
The colophon is a trademark of Multnomah Publishers, Inc.

Printed in the United States of America

For information:
MULTNOMAH PUBLISHERS, INC.
601 N. LARCH ST.
SISTERS, OREGON 97759

05 06 07 08 09 10—10 9 8 7 6 5 4 3 2 1 0

Contents

Extreme Measures

by Andy Stanley

O ver the past few years, television programmers have stumbled across an intriguing quirk of human nature: We love to watch people test their limits. First came the X Games, which basically takes all our childhood dares from the playground and molds them into professional sports. And if those physical tests weren't enough, next they invented a genre called "reality TV" to test the mental and emotional limits of willing contestants. At the same time, a new crop of animal shows emerged in which wild-eyed hosts contradict themselves by showing us just how close to a crocodile we should never get.

You see, there's something inside us that wants to explore what it's like to live on the edge. It's human nature to see how close we can get without going over. In fact, the trend of culture is to encourage us to max out financially, relationally, morally, and in our schedules. Whatever it is, just go for it!

But in the real world, that style of living is not sustainable for long. And as we're about to discover together, it's not what God had in mind for your life. Sooner or later as you follow Christ, He is going to lead you toward a life with margin…where relationships thrive, financial pressures dissipate, and peace reigns.

Getting there isn't always easy. It can mean facing some heart-wrenching challenges in the key areas of your life. But if you're willing to consider taking some extreme measures in the name of margin, you can begin to orchestrate your life to be a little less threatening and a lot more enjoyable and productive.

Less Is More

The message is all around us: Be all you can be! Go for the gusto! Take it to the extreme! From an early age, our culture encourages us to push the limits physically, emotionally, and experientially. Success, it seems, is determined by how much we can squeeze out of each and every opportunity in life.

But what happens when all those opportunities start to squeeze the life out of you? What should you do when the pace gets too hectic and the money gets too tight? Is it possible there's a flaw in our frenetic philosophy? Maybe more isn't always more?

In this session, we'll see how our common fear of missing out on life can lure us into a lifestyle that simply isn't sustainable. We'll reveal the four primary areas of life that are most likely to suffer. And we'll lay the groundwork for a strategy to help you identify the pitfalls in your life and regain control. When God created man, He created him with limits. And through the frenzy, God is quietly calling us back to a life of margin.

EXERCISE

STRESS-O-METER

Using a scale from 1 to 10, write a number to indicate the average level of stress you feel in each of the following categories of life. Write a "1" if you feel little or no stress, a "5" if you feel moderate to significant stress, and a "10" if you feel totally frazzled.

Schedule _____

Finances _____

Relationships _____

Spirituality _____

Career _____

Add up the five numbers to calculate your score. How many people in your group scored higher than 10? 15? 25? What is your group's average score?

" I try to take one day at a time, but sometimes several days attack me at once. "
—Jennifer Yane

VIDEO NOTES

From the video message, fill in the blanks:

1. Margin: An amount available beyond what is actually _____ ; the extra; reserves.

2. Margin is the space between our current _____ and our limits.

3. When margin begins to shrink…
   - _____ levels go up.
   - _____ narrows.
   - _____ suffer.

4. _____ happens in margin.

NOTES

DISCUSSION QUESTIONS

Take a few moments to discuss your answers to these questions with the group.

1. What does the world say about personal limits?
2. What are some examples of people running out of margin?
3. Why do we allow ourselves to live without margin?
4. What evidence do you see that God intended us to live with margin?
5. How does your current performance compare to your absolute limits?
6. In what areas are you living with the least amount of margin?

MILEPOSTS

- Our culture urges us to test our limits.
- God calls us to a life of margin.
- Margin is the space between our current performance and our limits.
- God created us with limits.

WHAT WILL YOU DO?

This week, take a personal inventory of your life. What are the activities that drive your schedule? What are the expenses that drive your finances? What relationships test you emotionally? What situations tempt you morally? If you could change one thing about your life, what change would result in the most significant increase in margin?

Schedule

Financial

Emotional

Moral

THINK ABOUT IT

Are there any common fears that have lured you into a present lifestyle that is unsustainable? What about the fear of missing out? The fear of falling behind? The fear of a missed opportunity? The fear of not mattering? Which of these fears do you experience the most? What truths can you remind yourself of when you find yourself succumbing to this fear?

CHANGING YOUR MIND

God created us with limits. Renew your mind by meditating on this important foundational principle.

"Man's days are determined;
you have decreed the number of his months
and have set limits he cannot exceed."

JOB 14:5

LAST WEEK...

We observed that while culture encourages us to live at our absolute limits, God is calling us to a life with margin. Lack of margin can lead to personal failure in our schedules, finances, emotions, and morals. By acknowledging that we are created with limits, we can begin the process of creating margin in our lives.

Downtime

Your schedule is often the area of your life with the least margin available. And as your calendar goes, so goes your life. If we are to allow God to lead us to a place of margin, we must first be willing to examine the principles that govern our schedules.

In the last session, we established that we have been created with limits. And that's especially true when it comes to our schedules. God put twenty-four hours in each day. And He put a certain number of days in each of our lives. But somehow, when it comes to our calendar, we often act as if we have unlimited time. And when time begins to run out, we begin to allow the urgent things to push aside the important things.

In this session, we'll discover that God not only gave us our time, He also has a plan for how we spend it. And the first step toward experiencing His plan—and the margin that comes with it—is to turn over control of our calendars to Him.

WHO CALLS THE SHOTS?

Think about your own schedule for a minute. Which of the following categories tends to dictate your calendar the most? Rank them in order, 1 being the most influential and 5 being the least.

___ Professional

___ Civic/social

___ Physical/recreational

___ Family/household

___ Religious/spiritual

Share your top two categories with the group.

> " A life spent in constant labor is a life wasted, save a man be such a fool as to regard a fulsome obituary notice as ample reward. "
> —George Jean Nathan

VIDEO NOTES

From the video message, fill in the blanks:

THE FACTS OF LIFE

1. Your time is _____ .
2. All of your time will be spent doing
   _____ .
3. _____ will determine how your time is
   spent.

CREATING MARGIN

1. Recognize that your days are _____ by
   God.
2. _____ accordingly.
3. Make time alone with _____ a priority.

NOTES

DISCUSSION QUESTIONS

Take a few moments to discuss your answers to these questions with the group.

1. What are some of the factors that determine how your time is spent?
2. Why do we tend to overlook God as a source of wisdom for our schedules?
3. What are some criteria you could use to help you determine the wise thing to do with regard to your schedule?
4. What are some of the things that compete for the first few moments of each day?
5. What might be different if your habit was to spend the first few moments of each day with God?

MILEPOSTS

■ Your time is limited.

■ Somebody will determine how you spend your time—it might as well be you.

■ Give God the "first fruits" of your time.

WHAT WILL YOU DO?

This week, try an experiment to gain greater margin in your schedule. Set aside the first minutes of your day to spend time with God. Whether it is three minutes or thirty minutes, whether you pray or read the Bible or something else, begin making time with God a priority in your life. Then watch to see if you have more or less margin this week.

THINK ABOUT IT

If you were to adopt a new schedule, only adding things based on your top priorities, what are some of the things you might need to subtract from your current schedule?

It may be helpful to think in terms of what you'd like your schedule to look like one year from now. That way you can allow your current commitments to run their course, enabling you to bow out more gracefully.

CHANGING YOUR MIND

Meditate on this verse throughout the week as a reminder to give your schedule to God daily and to seek His wisdom for each moment He entrusts to you.

Teach us to number our days aright,
that we may gain a heart of wisdom."

PSALM 90:12

LAST WEEK...

We saw that even the most basic principles about time are often overlooked. In the rush of everyday life, we can begin to believe that our lives will somehow be exceptions to the rules that govern time management. The key to creating margin in our calendars lies in identifying our priorities, starting with the priority of spending time before the Lord each day.

Quality vs. Quantity

When it comes to finances, there's one very simple factor that determines whether or not we have margin. And it's not income. Many people assume that their finances would improve if only they could increase their earning power. But if that's what you've been thinking, you could be cheating yourself out of the very prosperity you're seeking.

At first glance, God's principles on finances can either seem simplistic or counterintuitive. But if you're a follower of God, money is not about math. It's about a personal relationship with the God who controls it all...including yours.

In this session, we'll examine two definitions of financial margin and learn the identity of the two people who get robbed if you don't have it. And in the process, we'll discover that the real key to financial margin is not increasing the quantity, but paying attention to the quality of our stewardship over what we already have.

HALF FULL OR HALF EMPTY?

Think about your own finances for a moment. If you could wave a magic wand and change one thing about your current money situation, what would it be? Share your answer with the group.

E X E R C I S E

> " Today, there are three kinds of people: the have's, the have-not's, and the have-not-paid-for-what-they-have's. "
> —Earl Wilson

VIDEO NOTES

From the video message, fill in the blanks:

1. Cash sources minus cash _____ .
2. The amount of money you have left to spend as you desire after living expenses and _____ commitments are met.
3. The issue with financial margin is not income, it's _____ .
4. When there is no financial margin, you rob yourself and you rob _____ .

NOTES

DISCUSSION QUESTIONS

Take a few moments to discuss your answers to these questions with the group.

1. Why do people tend to spend as much as they make?
2. Have you ever felt like you were under a curse financially?
3. Why do we wait until we're in trouble financially to seek God's help?
4. In which area of your finances (spending or income) is it the most difficult to trust God?
5. What are the benefits of financial margin?
6. What is the relationship between financial margin and giving to God?

MILEPOSTS

■ Financial Margin: Cash sources minus cash uses.

■ The issue with financial margin is not income, it's lifestyle.

■ When there is no financial margin, you rob yourself and you rob God.

WHAT WILL YOU DO?

This week, take a look at your current financial situation. Specifically, think about the percentage of your income God would have you strategically give to fund His kingdom. Draw up a plan of when, where, and how much you will give.

THINK ABOUT IT

What criteria do you follow to determine if you will make a purchase or not? Is it as simple as whether or not you have the money or the credit or whether it seems "reasonable"? Based on the message of this session, briefly describe a few guidelines that can help you evaluate future purchases before you make them.

CHANGING YOUR MIND

Making God our first financial priority is counterintuitive. But it's a principle from Scripture we can embrace in faith. Meditate on this verse throughout the week to help you remember God's priorities for the money He entrusts to you.

"'Test me in this,' says the Lord Almighty,
'and see if I will not throw open the floodgates of
heaven and pour out so much blessing that you
will not have room enough for it.'"

MALACHI 3:10

LAST WEEK...

We saw that the key to financial margin is not increasing income, but controlling expenses. God's financial principles can seem counterintuitive. But following God with our finances is about trusting the person who owns it all anyway—God. When we lack financial margin, we rob ourselves and we rob God.

Reordering Your Finances

Everybody wants financial margin. But how do you get there? The demands of a typical lifestyle in our culture can challenge even the best salary. Monthly expenses eat up monthly income faster than you can say, "minimum payment."

For many Christians, it seems that something always keeps them from turning the corner financially. If it's not an unexpected repair bill or an interest charge, it's a temporary layoff or a pay cut. So when you're ready to take a step toward financial margin, where do you begin?

In this session, we'll unveil a four-step plan to add financial margin to your budget—regardless of your current circumstances. It includes strategies for eliminating debt, saving for the future, and experiencing greater peace in your finances right away. In addition, we'll see that behind every financial issue that arises in your life is a spiritual issue that God is inviting you to face.

EXERCISE

THE REAL ISSUE

Every financial issue is a spiritual issue in disguise. Which of
the following spiritual issues is most likely to impact the way
you manage your finances? Rank them in order.

___ Fear

___ Jealousy

___ Anger

___ Greed

___ Impatience

Share your top two answers with the group.

> " We can tell our values by
> looking at our checkbook stubs. "
> — Gloria Steinem

VIDEO NOTES

From the video message, fill in the blanks:

MARGIN PLANNING

1. Identify your annual available _____ .

    Annual income
    – Debt Payments
    – Taxes
    – Obligations
    = Available Income

2. Set margin _____ .

    Available Income
    – Giving Goal (%)
    – Savings Goal (%)
    = Consumable Income

3. Determine your _____ consumable income.

    Consumable Income
    ÷ 12
    = Monthly Consumable Income

4. Develop a _____ .

    Track where your money is going.
    Give something now (%).
    Save something now (%).
    Develop a debt retirement plan.
    Develop a lifestyle reduction plan/budget.

5. Money is always a _____ issue.

NOTES

DISCUSSION QUESTIONS

Take a few moments to discuss your answers to these questions with the group.

1. What would you do if your personal money manager failed to keep accurate records of your money?

2. Have you ever thought of yourself as the manager of someone else's money?

3. Given your unique personality, is bookkeeping effortless or laborious?

4. Which of the steps outlined in this session is the most challenging for you?

5. Which of the spiritual issues outlined in this session best describes you?

6. What step could you take this week to begin dealing with this issue?

MILEPOSTS

■ The way you handle money is a spiritual issue.

■ We are not owners, but stewards of God's money.

■ Financial margin is a natural by-product of good stewardship.

WHAT WILL YOU DO?

This week, sit down and calculate the first three steps outlined in the video session (Of course, you don't have to share your answers with the group!)

Available Income:

Consumable Income:

Monthly Consumable Income:

THINK ABOUT IT

The fourth step, "Develop a plan," involves several specific action items: Track where your money is going. Give something now (%). Save something now (%). Develop a debt retirement plan. Develop a lifestyle reduction plan/budget. Which of these items represents the toughest challenge for you personally? Why?

What is one step you can take this week to begin to address this item?

CHANGING YOUR MIND

Financial margin is the natural by-product of proper stewardship. Meditate on this verse to remind you that the money you possess is not your money, but God's money for you to manage.

So if you have not been trustworthy in handling worldly wealth, who will trust you with true riches?"

LUKE 16:11

LAST WEEK...

We unveiled a four-step plan to create financial margin. The plan involved calculating monthly consumable income and setting goals for giving, saving, and debt elimination. We also looked at the components of a good financial plan, beginning with a system for tracking what you spend.

A Time to Run

For the most part, Christians don't plan to sin. Nobody wakes up and says, "Today, I think I'll abandon my convictions and act immorally so I can experience some guilt and consequences." When Christians sin, it's usually because they don't plan *not to*. Once again, we need margin to keep us from venturing into territory we mean to avoid.

This is especially true when it comes to sexual sin. Sexual temptation can be one of the most powerful forces a person will face. And it's also one of the most devastating. One mistake has the potential to scar us physically, spiritually, and emotionally. In fact, according to the Bible, sexual sin is in a category all by itself.

In this session, we'll see what it looks like when God calls us to a life of margin in the area of sexual morality. Instead of seeing how close we can get without going over the line, we'll examine some practical strategies for creating margin that encourages sexual purity. And as we're about to discover, it's not always enough just to walk away. Sometimes you have to run.

EXERCISE

WHAT DO YOU HAVE TO LOSE?

What are some things a person might lose as a result of becoming involved in sexual immorality? Give examples.

In light of such severe consequences, why do people still test the limits?

> *" There is nothing like early promiscuous sex for dispelling life's bright mysterious expectations. "*
> —Iris Murdoch

VIDEO NOTES

From the video message, fill in the blanks:

1. Everybody has moral _____ .

2. Our temptation is to live right on the

    _____ .

3. Sexual sin is in a category of its _____ .

4. Poor moral decisions affect a person

    _____ .

NOTES

DISCUSSION QUESTIONS

Take a few moments to discuss your answers to these questions with the group.

1. What are some examples of the ways our culture baits us to live without sexual margin?

2. What are some of the ways our culture turns against those who go "too far"?

3. What do you think it means to sin against your own body?

4. What might you lose if you experience moral failure in your life?

5. What are some practical measures you can take to flee?

MILEPOSTS

- Everybody has moral limits.

- Our temptation is to live right on the line.

- Sexual sin is in a category of its own.

WHAT WILL YOU DO?

Depending on your situation in life, there are some important boundaries you need to draw in order to create moral margin. Using the following guidelines, briefly describe how you will determine your own margin.

CREATING MORAL MARGIN

Teens: Before you find yourself in a potentially compromising situation, you need to decide how far you will go sexually.

Singles: The more active you've been sexually, the higher your standards need to be.

Married: It is often helpful to look at things from your spouse's perspective. How far would you want your spouse to go in order to protect himself or herself from sexual temptation?

THINK ABOUT IT

Drawing boundaries might mean taking some extreme measures. It could be awkward or uncomfortable. Seatbelts aren't always convenient, but they save lives. Similarly, the moral margin you will gain is worth the cost. In the space below, describe the price you anticipate paying for taking steps to create moral margin.

Is it worth it? Why?

CHANGING YOUR MIND

When it comes to this issue, sometimes it's uncomfortable to be bold. But you can't afford to be less than firm in your convictions. Meditate on this verse this week as an encouragement to be ready to flee.

"Flee from sexual immorality. All other sins a man commits are outside his body, but he who sins sexually sins against his own body."

1 CORINTHIANS 6:18–19

LAST WEEK...

We examined the importance of margin in the area of sexual immorality. When it comes to this subject, we all have limits. Culture entices us to limits that are unsafe—especially when you consider that sexual sin is in a category by itself. The best way to deal with sexual temptation is simply to run away.

Finding Professional Margin

Of all the areas of life where you can create margin, none has a more profound effect than in your work. Professional margin, if you can create it, has a ripple effect on every other area of your life. Work is the least negotiable part of your schedule. Work also paints your financial picture. Therefore, margin on your calendar and in your finances is largely dependent on your ability to achieve margin professionally.

Fortunately, the formula for professional margin is simple. In fact, it comes from one of the oldest principles in Scripture. And it is modeled by people like Moses. Although you can't get there overnight, you can get an instant picture of where you need to be.

In this final session, we'll reveal the secret that enabled Moses to multiply his productivity while reducing his effort. You'll learn how to identify the one thing about you that can make you indispensable to your employer. And you'll see how to prioritize your efforts to achieve maximum productivity and create professional margin.

EXERCISE

BALL AND CHAIN

Most of us have a sweet spot at work—a skill or function that makes us indispensable. Unfortunately, we can spend vast portions of time doing other things. Sometimes red tape and paperwork are unavoidable; but they can be like a ball and chain, limiting productivity. We should be strategic about how we spend our time. Approximately how much of your time at work is spent performing the skills that make you indispensable?

How much is spent on mundane or meaningless routines?

Even when the urgent is good, the good can keep you from your best.
—Helen Keller

VIDEO NOTES

From the video message, fill in the blanks:

1. If you continue to say yes to everything that comes your way, your _____ suffers.
2. Most people are really _____ at one or two things.
3. Of all the things that are expected of us, only a couple make a real _____ to the organization.
4. Moses had the courage and the humility to _____ .
5. Professional margin can be summed up in the word _____ .

NOTES

DISCUSSION QUESTIONS

Take a few moments to discuss your answers to these questions with the group.

1. What are some of the ways people do "whatever it takes" to get the job done?
2. What are some of the professional tasks you do that don't really add to the bottom line?
3. Professionally, what are some of the things you do better than anyone else?
4. What are some ways you can marry your skills with specific needs to make yourself indispensable?
5. Describe the ideal job situation for leveraging your strengths and delegating your weaknesses.
6. What is one step you can take this week to begin the process of moving toward such a professional situation?

MILEPOSTS

■ If you continue to say yes to everything that comes your way, your productivity suffers.

■ When you can marry your skill set with your greatest area of impact, you create professional margin.

■ Play to your strengths; delegate to your weaknesses.

WHAT WILL YOU DO?

This week, write a detailed job description designed to create alignment between the following three parameters:

1. Your definition of personal success
2. Your company's mission
3. Your primary skill set

Ideal job description:

THINK ABOUT IT

What are some of your responsibilities that are NOT your strengths? List them here.

Why is it important for you to move away from these over the long term?

CHANGING YOUR MIND

Meditating on Scripture is the best way to align our hearts with God's principles. Memorize this passage of Scripture this week as a reminder to focus on what you do best.

"Moses listened to his father-in-law and did everything he said. He chose capable men from all Israel and made them leaders of the people, officials over thousands, hundreds, fifties and tens."

Exodus 18:24–25

LEADER'S GUIDE

So, You're the Leader...

Is that intimidating? Perhaps exciting? No doubt you have some mental pictures of what it will look like, what you will say, and how it will go. Before you get too far into the planning process, there are some things you should know about leading a small-group discussion. We've compiled some tried and true techniques here to help you.

BASICS ABOUT LEADING

1. **Don't teach...facilitate**—Perhaps you've been in a Sunday school class or Bible study in which the leader could answer any question and always had something interesting to say. It's easy to think you need to be like that too. Relax. You don't. Leading a small group is quite different. Instead of being the featured act at the party, think of yourself as the host or hostess behind the scenes. Your primary job is to create an environment where people feel comfortable and to keep the meeting generally on track. Your party is most successful when your guests do most of the talking.

2. **Cultivate discussion**—It's also easy to think that the meeting lives or dies by *your* ideas. In reality, what makes a small-group meeting successful are the ideas of everyone in the group. The most valuable thing you can do is to get people to share their thoughts. That's how the relationships in your group will grow and thrive. Here's a rule: The impact of your study material will typically never exceed the impact of the relationships through which it was studied. The more meaningful the relationships, the more meaningful the study. In a sterile environment, even the best material is suppressed.

3. **Point to the material**—A good host or hostess gets the party going by offering delectable hors d'oeuvres and beverages. You too should be ready to serve up "delicacies" from the material. Sometimes you will simply read the discussion questions and invite everyone to respond. At other times, you may encourage someone to share his own ideas. Remember, some of the best treats are the ones your guests

will bring to the party. Go with the flow of the meeting, and be ready to pop out of the kitchen as needed.

4. **Depart from the material**—A talented ministry team has carefully designed this study for your small group. But that doesn't mean you should follow every part word for word. Knowing how and when to depart from the material is a valuable art. Nobody knows more about your people than you do. The narratives, questions, and exercises are here to provide a framework for discovery. However, every group is motivated differently. Sometimes the best way to start a small-group discussion is simply to ask, "Does anyone have a personal insight or revelation he'd like to share from this week's material?" Then sit back and listen.

5. **Stay on track**—Conversation is like the currency of a small-group discussion. The more interchange, the healthier the "economy." However, you need to keep your objectives in mind. If your goal is to have a meaningful experience with this material, then you should

make sure the discussion is contributing to that end. It's easy to get off on a tangent. Be prepared to interject politely and refocus the group. You may need to say something like, "Excuse me, we're obviously all interested in this subject; however, I just want to make sure we cover all the material for this week."

6. **Above all, pray**—The best communicators are the ones who manage to get out of God's way enough to let Him communicate *through* them. That's important to keep in mind. Books don't teach God's Word; neither do sermons or group discussions. God Himself speaks into the hearts of men and women, and prayer is our vital channel to communicate directly with Him. Cover your efforts in prayer. You don't just want God present at your meeting, you want Him to direct it.

We hope you find these suggestions helpful. And we hope you enjoy leading this study. You will find additional guides and suggestions for each session in the Leader's Guide notes that follow.

Leader's Guide Notes

SESSION 1—LESS IS MORE

KEY POINT

Our culture, as well as human nature itself, encourages us to live as close to the edge as possible. But it's not without consequences. Behind our insatiable desire for more is the simple fear of missing out. However God has designed each of us with limits. He intended us to identify our priorities and build margin into our lives. There are four key areas of life in which we must learn to apply this principle.

EXERCISE—STRESS-O-METER

The purpose of this opening exercise is to give participants a personal connection to the material. Stress is something that impacts everyone. As this exercise suggests, this study explores principles that can be leveraged to improve the way stress is managed and avoided in our everyday lives.

VIDEO NOTES

1. Margin: An amount available beyond what is actually <u>needed</u>; the extra; reserves.

2. Margin is the space between our current <u>performance</u> and our limits.

3. When margin begins to shrink…

   ■ <u>Stress</u> levels go up.

   ■ <u>Focus</u> narrows.

   ■ <u>Relationships</u> suffer.

4. <u>Relationship</u> happens in margin.

NOTES FOR DISCUSSION QUESTIONS

1. What does the world say about personal limits? The world encourages us to ignore and challenge personal limits. However, this philosophy overlooks the reality that God created us with limits. We should not live our lives ignorant of God's intentions.

2. What are some examples of people running out
   of margin?

   In order to address this problem, it is helpful
   to revisit examples of how it can impact our
   lives. This question can elicit personal stories
   from group members or examples from the
   world at large.

3. Why do we allow ourselves to live without
   margin?

   Before we can identify long-term solutions to
   the problem of margin, it is helpful to identify
   the reasons we deplete margin in the first
   place. This question will prompt participants
   to consider our natural tendencies and how
   to reverse them.

4. What evidence do you see that God intended
   us to live with margin?

   In response to this question, you may start
   the discussion by citing a few of the more
   obvious examples of man's limitations—our

need for sleep, our decreasing physical strength as we age, and so on.

5. How does your current performance compare to your absolute limits?

This question is a measure of how much margin a person has in his life. If your current performance is at your absolute limit, there is no margin. If current performance is below the limit, there is margin. Rather than suggesting a subpar performance, this may actually suggest better longevity and quality of life.

6. In what areas are you living with the least amount of margin?

The purpose of this question is to identify the most problematic areas so that they can be addressed more specifically in the sessions to come.

WHAT WILL YOU DO?

When lack of margin is a problem, it is usually because an activity or practice has been given inordinate influence in your life. Activities have the potential to drive our calendars; purchases have the potential to drive our finances. When we identify the major sources of conflict, we identify the areas we need to address.

THINK ABOUT IT

Encourage participants to identify the fears that cause them to live without margin. By identifying their fears, they will begin to address not only the symptoms, but also the underlying problems. By identifying the truth, they will learn how to combat their fears.

SESSION 2—DOWNTIME

KEY POINT

This session focuses on time management and the impact of margin in a person's calendar. It's easy to allow "urgent" activities to dictate our schedules, but living within our limits requires that we be guided by what's "important" instead. Our calendar gains margin when we allow God to direct it…and that begins with making it a priority to carve out time with Him each day.

EXERCISE—WHO CALLS THE SHOTS?

In every person's calendar, there is usually a key category that takes precedent over all the others. It may be work, family, the gym, or friendships. Without realizing it, we can allow these things to dictate the pace of our lives. This exercise will help participants identify which category dictates their schedules.

VIDEO NOTES

The Facts of Life

1. Your time is <u>limited</u>.
2. All of your time will be spent doing <u>something</u>.
3. <u>Somebody</u> will determine how your time is spent.

Creating Margin

4. Recognize that your days are <u>numbered</u> by God.
5. <u>Prioritize</u> accordingly.
6. Make time alone with <u>God</u> a priority.

NOTES FOR DISCUSSION QUESTIONS

1. What are some of the factors that determine how your time is spent?
   In the undertone of this entire session is the question, "What would happen if you took complete control of your calendar and were

no longer locked in to certain activities?"
Many people simply get up, go to work, go
home, and so on, just because they think
they're supposed to. Instead, we should look
to God and be willing to rethink how we live
and why.

2. Why do we tend to overlook God as a source
   of wisdom for our schedules?
   What does God know about your daily activities and responsibilities? When it comes right
   down to it, many of us just assume that God
   doesn't have strong opinions about the
   details. This question will prompt participants to consider the obvious: God is a
   source of wisdom here too.

3. What are some criteria you could use to help
   you determine the wise thing to do with regard
   to your schedule?
   This is an important thought to entertain.
   Unless we think about how we design our
   schedules, we can simply default to a process
   that doesn't reflect our priorities. Pondering

this question will help participants feel the
need for a good strategy in this area.

4. What are some of the things that compete for
   the first few moments of each day?
   Encourage participants to analyze their priorities when it comes the beginning of the
   day. What is it that they value in the morning? Beating traffic, sleeping longer, the
   morning paper?

5. What might be different if your habit was to
   spend the first few moments of each day with
   God?
   There is no right or wrong answer to this question. Participants will likely envision a number
   of positive outcomes from taking this step.

WHAT WILL YOU DO?

The purpose of this exercise is to cause participants to take the first step in creating margin in their schedules—to carve out time for God. By beginning to give God their first moments, they set themselves up to allow God to focus their energy during the day.

THINK ABOUT IT

A key part of designing a new schedule is facing up to the fact that we must be willing to say no to certain activities. This exercise will help participants begin the process of saying goodbye to certain activities and embracing a life of margin.

SESSION 3—QUALITY VS. QUANTITY

KEY POINT

This is the first of two sessions on financial margin. While the next session deals with specific strategies for creating margin, this session focuses on some important attitudes of the heart that must be embraced in order to experience true freedom in the area of finances. Having plenty of money does not make someone financially free; understanding God's perspective on money does.

EXERCISE—HALF FULL OR HALF EMPTY?

When we think of solutions to financial problems, most people automatically think of adding money to the equation. But the solution can also be achieved by reducing expenses—although we often convince ourselves that's not an option. Based on your answers in this exercise, which type of solution did the people in your group come up with automatically?

VIDEO NOTES

1. Cash sources minus cash <u>uses</u>.
2. The amount of money you have left to spend as you desire after living expenses and <u>mandatory</u> commitments are met.
3. The issue with financial margin is not income, it's <u>lifestyle</u>.
4. When there is no financial margin, you rob yourself and you rob <u>God</u>.

NOTES FOR DISCUSSION QUESTIONS

1. Why do people tend to spend as much as they make?

   There are several ways to answer this question, but all point to the issues behind our behaviors. We spend because we want and because we assume it's ours to spend. In order to experience margin, both of these issues must be reconciled with God's truth about money.

2. Have you ever felt like you were under a curse financially?

   The purpose of this question is to generate dialogue regarding the potential conse-quences of ignoring God's instruction in the area of finances.

3. Why do we wait until we're in trouble financially to seek God's help?

   Regardless of how this question is answered, it serves to highlight the futility of avoiding God as a source of help and wisdom for finances. If He is a suitable source of help in times of trouble, how much more so when we are starting out?

4. In which area of your finances (spending or income) is it the most difficult to trust God?

   Whether controlling our spending or seeking sources of income, it's easy to forget that God has authority over all our circumstances and can be our everyday. This question will help partici-pants identify specific areas in which they may be struggling to apply God's financial wisdom.

5. What are the benefits of financial margin?

Vision is often the missing ingredient in our faith. Unless we can picture the outcome of trusting God with a particular situation, it can be very difficult to take the necessary steps of faith...or even to identify what they are. This question will help the people in your group develop vision.

6. What is the relationship between financial margin and giving to God?

Increasing your financial margin begins by giving to God. When you give to fund God's kingdom, you invite God into your finances, and He will increase your financial margin. As you have more financial margin, you are able to give more to God.

WHAT WILL YOU DO?

The thrust of this week's session is that financial margin begins when you put God first. You can put God first by setting aside a percentage of your income to fund His kingdom. While in the Old Testament 10 percent was considered the tithe, in the New Testament we are not locked into a specific percentage or number. Everyone needs to spend time with God to determine what God would have him give.

THINK ABOUT IT

To get to the bottom of our spending problems, it's important to consider why we purchase in the first place. Many of us lack good criteria for justifying our purchases. Instead, we approve our spending based on comparison with others or because we feel a strong desire to own something. This exercise will help participants realize that clear criteria will lead to tangible control over spending.

SESSION 4—REORDERING YOUR FINANCES

KEY POINT

This session is the second of two chapters on financial margin. In this session, we explore some very practical things to do in order to begin to create financial margin. In particular, this session outlines four steps to take to ensure there is extra cash left over at the end of each month now...and when you retire.

EXERCISE—THE REAL ISSUE

Each of these spiritual issues can have a direct impact on our finances. And each one is explained throughout this series. The purpose of this exercise is to reinforce the idea that financial issues are not simply a matter of needing more money.

Video Notes

1. Identify your annual available <u>income</u>.
   Annual income
   – Debt Payments
   – Taxes
   – Obligations
   = Available Income

2. Set margin <u>goals</u>.
   Available Income
   – Giving Goal (%)
   – Savings Goal (%)
   = Consumable Income

3. Determine your <u>monthly</u> consumable income.
   Consumable Income
   ÷ 12
   = Monthly Consumable Income

4. Develop a <u>plan</u>.
   Track where your money is going.
   Give something now (%).
   Save something now (%).
   Develop a debt retirement plan.
   Develop a lifestyle reduction plan/budget.

5. Money is always a <u>spiritual</u> issue.

NOTES FOR DISCUSSION QUESTIONS

1. What would you do if your personal money manager failed to keep accurate records of your money?

   The main point of this question is to allow participants to spend a minute thinking about things from God's perspective. Whether we like it or not, understand it or not, believe it or not, God has assigned us to be managers of a portion of His money. Part of that assignment is to know where the money is going each month.

2. Have you ever thought of yourself as the manager of someone else's money?

   This question builds on the previous question, making sure that participants apply the analogy. For many people, this is a new concept. Often, it is so enlightening that people are instantly empowered to begin viewing their finances from God's perspective. Be sure each person in your group has a chance to grasp this idea.

3. Given your unique personality, is bookkeeping effortless or laborious?

Our unique personality type can make it either easier or more difficult to manage money. While this is never acceptable as an excuse, we should be aware of our individual tendencies. If money management does not come easily, we must agree to work harder at it.

4. Which of the steps outlined in this session is the most challenging for you?

For every participant, some steps will be easier than others. It will be helpful to recognize up front where we are likely to lose momentum. Encourage those in your group to not lose heart when they struggle with one or more of these steps. Remind them that God is working behind the scenes to use finances as a tool to shape our spiritual growth.

5. Which of the spiritual issues outlined in this session best describes you?

This question is designed to help participants personalize the issues described in the video message. The better we know ourselves, the more adeptly we can pursue spiritual growth and achieve financial margin.

6. What step could you take this week to begin dealing with this issue?

   It is important to leave this session with at least one specific action step to take this week. Make sure each person is able to articulate his plan upon leaving this session. You may also want to follow up next week to ensure that each participant has followed through. The first step is often the most difficult. Your encouragement could mean the difference between a message appreciated and a message appropriated.

WHAT WILL YOU DO?

The content of this session is rich with application. To make sure the people in your group really apply the material, this exercise walks them through the first three steps. Privacy is vital. Remind them that they will not be asked to share their personal financial information with anyone in the group.

THINK ABOUT IT

The final step of the application involves ongoing management in several areas. Once again, if each person is able to anticipate the toughest part of the assignment, he or she will be better prepared to complete it despite the obstacles.

SESSION 5—A TIME TO RUN

KEY POINT

When we speak of morality throughout this session, we are referring to sexual morality in particular. Many Christians think of sexual morality simply in terms of dos and don'ts. And therein lies the problem. Margin is a concept that applies to morality as well. Rather than only measuring whether we've done something or not, we should measure how close we will allow ourselves to get in the first place. The extra margin ensures that when we fall, we don't fall into sin.

EXERCISE—WHAT DO YOU HAVE TO LOSE?

The consequences of sin can be tragic, painful, and sad. But for the person pursuing moral margin, they actually have a positive side. Potential consequences provide tremendous motivation for us to live with purity. No human is beyond the potential to sin. It can be helpful to remind ourselves just what's at stake.

Video Notes

1. Everybody has moral <u>limits</u>.
2. Our temptation is to live right on the <u>line</u>.
3. Sexual sin is in a category of its <u>own</u>.
4. Poor moral decisions affect a person <u>psychologically</u>.

Notes for Discussion Questions

1. What are some examples of the ways our culture baits us to live without sexual margin? In modern America, there is no end to the examples of how culture portrays sex. As participants share their examples, it can provide a sobering realization of the moral state of the world. Unless we are aware of the current, we can be swept along before we know it.

2. What are some of the ways our culture turns against those who go "too far"?

As is pointed out during the video message, there is an ironic twist to the culture's sexual bait. This punitive side of culture actually works to our advantage, reminding us that the invitation to illicit sexual pleasure is really a facade. It leads only to complication, guilt, pain, or worse.

3. What do you think it means to sin against your own body?

It is important for each participant to realize the uniqueness of sexual sin. This question is designed to ensure that each person wrestles with the idea for a moment.

4. What might you lose if you experience moral failure in your life?

As discussed in the opening exercise, it is often very motivating to consider what's at stake if we sin sexually. You may remind your group that sexual sin also tends to escalate from "small" sins to bigger ones. As a result,

even small compromises must be taken very
seriously as they could spiral out of control
and lead to disaster.

5. What are some practical measures you can take
   to flee?
   At the end of the day, we all need specific
   steps we can take to establish moral margin.
   This question helps each person in the group
   personalize the message for his or her own
   unique situation.

WHAT WILL YOU DO?

Each person faces a unique situation. It is important to
spend adequate time developing a viable strategy for creating moral margin. Satan is a real being who is scheming to
destroy our lives. God, through His Holy Spirit, enables us
to identify and apply wise strategies to emerge victorious in
spite of the enemy. But we have to approach it like the war
that it is.

THINK ABOUT IT

Finally, it is important to recognize that there is a price to pay for establishing moral margin. Share this openly with your group so that everyone knows what to expect. That way they won't be discouraged when it happens. Use this exercise to help your group members anticipate some of the obstacles that may tempt them to shrink back from their resolve to create moral margin.

SESSION 6—FINDING PROFESSIONAL MARGIN

KEY POINT

We spend more waking hours at work than anywhere else. Therefore, creating professional margin impacts every other aspect of life. Professional margin means accomplishing more with less effort so that our jobs don't encroach inordinately into the other areas of life. Surprisingly, the Bible contains some very practical advice about how to be more productive at work.

EXERCISE—BALL AND CHAIN

This exercise is designed to get participants thinking about a concept that is vital to the message of this session. God has gifted each of us with certain skills and talents that are unique to us. Our strengths in these respective areas offer indications of where He would have us focus our attention for maximum effectiveness. When we go with our God-given strengths, we set ourselves up to have margin professionally.

VIDEO NOTES

1. If you continue to say yes to everything that comes your way, your <u>productivity</u> suffers.
2. Most people are really <u>good</u> at one or two things.
3. Of all the things that are expected of us, only a couple make a real <u>difference</u> to the organization.
4. Moses had the courage and the humility to <u>listen</u>.
5. Professional margin can be summed up in the word <u>focus</u>.

NOTES FOR DISCUSSION QUESTIONS

1. What are some of the ways people do "whatever it takes" to get the job done?
   This question points to a common problem that arises when we are driven professionally. Professionalism is good, but when work accomplishments are elevated too much, our lives

can fall out of balance. Spending some time reviewing answers to this question will help sensitize the group to this potential.

2. What are some of the professional tasks you do that don't really add to the bottom line?

We usually don't notice a loss of productivity because it's gradual and we don't give it much thought. This question is designed to make us give it some thought. Remember, almost every task at work is necessary; but there are some tasks that add very little to the bottom line. This question is not necessarily asking for examples of tasks that should be eliminated altogether, but ones that might be candidates for us to manage better.

3. Professionally, what are some of the things you do better than anyone else?

In a manner similar to the question above, we should also analyze our workload to identify the greatest contributions we make in the workplace. Again, it's not necessarily so that we can eliminate everything else entirely, but so that we can begin managing our time to focus on the most important parts of work.

4. What are some ways you can marry your skills with specific needs to make yourself indispensable?

In questions 3 and 4, we identified the strongest skill sets. But having skill is only part of the equation. God has given us skills for the purpose of performing good works that He has prepared for us (Ephesians 2:10). This question will prompt participants to match their skills with areas of need.

5. Describe the ideal job situation for leveraging your strengths and delegating your weaknesses.

For this question, encourage the people in your group not to be limited by their current jobs, but to create imaginary jobs that fully exploit their potential. It may seem unrealistic, but it will give participants valuable targets and reference points for making decisions that will shape their futures professionally.

6. What is one step you can take this week to begin the process of moving toward such a professional situation?

   Again, the idea is not to quit the current job and search for the dream job. But over time, we can begin taking small steps that make our current jobs more and more like the situation in which we would be most productive. People who attempt such steps are often surprised at how closely their jobs can resemble the jobs of their dreams.

WHAT WILL YOU DO?

As described in the video message, these three criteria form the blueprint for an ideal job description. First, each person should prayerfully seek a clear understanding of what total success means to him personally (for some, it may mean earning the most money, or making the world a better place). Second, he should focus on the company's mission and be able to envision contributing to it. Third, he should be able to anticipate how his unique skills can be leveraged to accomplish the first and second objectives with maximum efficiency.

THINK ABOUT IT

Last, and perhaps most importantly, it is vital to identify the "don't do" tasks. Time is limited. In order to create margin, we must be able to eliminate tasks that are not part of the model for efficiency. Like we've said, we usually don't give much thought to what we're doing. Identifying these tasks once and for all will help us recognize when we are starting to drift off course. We usually can't eliminate these tasks immediately, but over time we can make significant improvements.

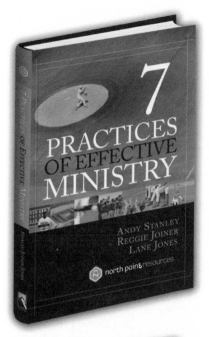

7 Practices of Effective Ministry

by Andy Stanley, Reggie Joiner, and Lane Jones

ISBN 1-59052-373-3

Rethink Your Ministry Game Plan
Succeeding in sports means victory, winning! But what does it mean in your ministry? An insightful and entertaining parable for every church leader who yearns for a more simplified approach to ministry.

Creating Community

by Andy Stanley and Bill Willits

ISBN 1-59052-396-2

Form Small Groups That Succeed
To build a healthy, thriving small-group environment you need a plan. Here are five proven principles from one of the most successful small-group ministry churches in the country. Learn them, implement them, and empower God's people to truly do life together.

north point resources

Parental Guidance Required
by Andy Stanley and Reggie Joiner
DVD: ISBN 1-59052-378-4
Study Guide: ISBN 1-59052-381-4

Influence Your Child's Future
Our lives are shaped by relationships, experiences, and decisions. Therefore, our priority as parents should be to enhance our child's relationship with us, advance our child's relationship with God, and influence our child's relationship with those outside the home.

Discovering God's Will
by Andy Stanley
DVD: ISBN 1-59052-380-6
Study Guide: ISBN 1-59052-379-2

Make Decisions with Confidence
God has a personal vision for your life and He wants you to know it even more than you do. Determining God's will can be a difficult process, especially when we need to make a decision in a hurry. In this series Andy Stanley leads us through God's providential, moral, and personal will.

The Best Question Ever
by Andy Stanley
DVD: ISBN 1-59052-463-2
Study Guide: ISBN 1-59052-462-4

Foolproof Your Life
When it comes to sorting out the complexities of each unique situation we face, only wisdom can reveal the best path. The question posed here will empower you to make regretless decisions every time.

north point resources